AIRFIELD FO(

WATTC

by Geoff Gardin(

Situated close to the small town of Watton, the airfield of the same name was twenty miles west of Norwich. The land, flat, well drained and on the edge of an area known as Breckland, was mainly arable and was well known for mushrooms, which grew profusely. In Anglo-Saxon times the town of Thetford, eleven miles (17.7km.) away, was the capital of East Anglia, important as a centre for the wool trade.

Construction of Watton airfield began in the Royal Air Force expansion period just before the outbreak of the Second World War. Built by John Laing & Son, Watton was a typical permanent Station of that period, with four large 'C' type hangars fronted by a large tarmac apron and with perimeter tracks surrounding a grass landing field. A watch office (control tower) of the standard 'Fort' type was positioned between

hanga. NCOs and airmen were spacious, comfortable and easily accessible, unlike the dispersed Nissen hut sites of hastily-built wartime airfields.

On 2 January 1939 an advance party of four officers, one sergeant and twenty-three airmen arrived from Feltwell and the Station was placed under the command of Wg. Cdr. F. J. Vincent four days later. At the time the Station was under a blanket of snow and the only working telephone was in the adjutant's office.

The Sergeants' Mess came into use on 3 February and the Station officially opened next day. Originally Watton was chosen for the bombers of 6 Group, Bomber Command, but at the last minute it was allocated to 2 Group, which had been raised on 20 March 1936 with headquarters at

Watton from the air on 4 October 1939, showing the lines painted on the grass to simulate hedges and trees. This ploy may have disguised the airfield but it did nothing to hide the hangars and other buildings when this picture was taken in bright sunlight. [P. H. T. Green collection]

Watton's original Watch Office, a concrete structure type 207/36, and a 'C' type hangar form the background to visiting Magister P2384, probably of Station Flight Northolt, in 1939.
[J. Reardon]

Abingdon and was organised into five wings. Watton was planned as the base for 79 Wing, consisting of two Blenheim light day bomber squadrons, 21 and 34.

The first three Blenheims Mk.I and an advance party of 21 Sqn. arrived from Eastchurch under Flt . Lt . Gibson and 34 Sqn. moved in from Upper Heyford on 23 February 1939. On 17 March Wg. Cdr. Vincent was promoted to Group Captain and on the same day the first Blenheim crashed at Watton, the crew escaping unhurt.

Retired Wg. Cdr. Peter Meston was a young pilot on 21 Sqn. as well as the squadron adjutant. He recalls that he flew Blenheim Mk.I L1350 to Watton on 27 February to see how preparations were proceeding for the squadron move. He was involved in the first Blenheim crash at

Watton and recalls the incident. *"It was a dreadful day with a high wind and very bumpy. I was ordered to give dual instruction to a very experienced sergeant pilot who was converting onto Blenheims. I queried the wisdom of this in view of the weather but was overuled by the CO. On the first landing, just short of the airfield we hit a very bad gust and the port wing dropped about 45 degrees. The text book correction for a slight drop of a wing was to apply opposite rudder. The sergeant did just that and induced a side slip. I grabbed the controls and tried to pick up the wing on the ailerons. Given two or three feet more I might have succeeded. However we hit the ground going sideways and wrote off the aircraft. Later I was blamed for giving dual in these conditions!"*

He also noted a series of engine

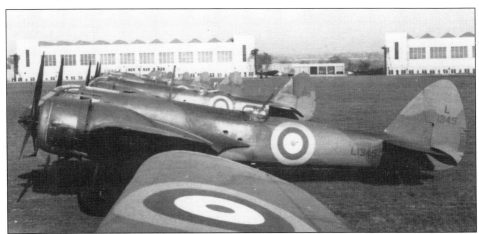

A line-up of Blenheims I of 21 Sqn. at Watton, probably soon after the Station opened. L1345, nearest the camera, was transferred to 90 Sqn., 104 Sqn. and 13 OTU before being sent to Finland on 21 February 1940. L1350, second in line, also moved to 90 Sqn., with which it crash-landed at Upwood on 17 November 1939.
[P. H. T. Green collection]

failures at other Stations which often had fatal consequences. *"Watton seemed to avoid this hazard until when I was flying at 3-4000 feet my port engine failed. With this amount of height in hand I was not greatly worried. We had never been instructed in single engine flying. However, I found I could just maintain height and headed for home. In those days airfields had left hand circuits so my next ploy was to see the effect of a left turn (into my bad engine). The aircraft promptly swung into a descending turn. I then tried turning into my good engine and found this was possible. I did a right hand circuit, did a high approach, put my wheels and flaps down late and closed the good engine late to do a full glide approach. This enabled me to trim the aircraft to neutral and make a successful landing. This was reported to Central Flying School and became the basis for a standard single engine approach. The reason that 21 Sqn. suffered from very few engine failures was that Flt. Sgt. Jones insisted on turning over engines daily. The cause of the trouble was that lead crystals could build up in the valve stems and finally jam the valves. "Chiefy" Jones action prevented this"*.

Peter Meston had another frightening experience during a practice exercise over Watton. He recalls *"21 Sqn. was a low-level day bomber squadron. Bombs were fused with an 11 second delay. Group decided they would like to see how many aircraft they could get to bomb the target in 11 seconds. I never saw the point of this as the last aircraft would be blown up the bomb of the first aircraft. A tent was placed on the airfield and nine Blenheims took part. I was number nine. This was purely a timing exercise. The idea was to pass as close as possible to the aircraft in front of you. We came in at all angles and eight aircraft passed successfully. I came in, hit everyone's slip stream and ended up going over the hangars upside down! I continued the roll and landed with the other aircraft. The AOC was not amused and I was reprimanded but excused when I explained the situation. We never tried the exercise again"*.

34 Sqn. did not stay long at Watton. A young airman, Jack Reardon, had just completed his trade training at St. Athan in South Wales and was posted as ground crew to 34 Sqn. in mid-1939. Arriving in the town and not certain where to go, he enquired from a local *"Where is the RAF station?"*. *"Are you going to 34 Squadron?"* he was asked. Jack nodded and the local replied *"You'll be going to Singapore then!"* Apparently this was common knowledge among the townsfolk. The man's prediction came to pass and 34 Sqn. left Watton for Singapore on 16 August. The first eight Blenheims took off and were escorted as far as the UK coast by the Station Commander, Gp. Capt. Vincent. Groundcrews embarked from Southampton on the troopship SS Neuralia, arriving in Colombo on the day war broke out.

Replacing 34 Sqn. at Watton on 22 August 1939 came 82 Sqn. from Cranfield. Equipped with Blenheim Mk.Is early in 1938, the squadron had received the improved Mk.IV just before arriving at Watton. Wg. Cdr. S. H. Ware took command of the squadron in July. War was now just a few weeks away and the two squadrons were working up to prepare for whatever the future held.

L1413 was a Blenheim I of 34 Sqn., seen here at Watton in the summer of 1939, before the squadron left for Malaya. This Blenheim, here carrying the 1938-series LB code, was lost when the Japanese over-ran Malaya in January 1942. [P. H. T. Green collection]

Bill Denney had enlisted in the RAF in November 1938 as a Clerk (General Duties). A very competent and intelligent airman, he was later to reach commissioned rank. He was posted after initial training to Eastchurch and 21 Sqn. and moved with the main party in March 1939 to Watton. On 3 September 1939 he was playing tennis when a runner arrived to tell him to report to the orderly room. There he found the Adjutant attempting to decipher a secret signal, apparently using the wrong deciphering equipment. When Bill had deciphered it correctly the message read *"Great Britain is at war with Germany only — repeat, Germany only"*.

Watton at war

Mobilisation orders had already been received in cypher on 1 September and next day the "scatter" plan was executed. The idea was to disperse squadrons to bases further inland or in some cases merely around the Station perimeter in order to present a less concentrated target for enemy bombers. 21 Sqn. dispersed at Watton and 82 Sqn. left for Horsham St Faith. When war was officially declared 2 Group ordered 21 Sqn. to Sealand and 82 Sqn. to Netheravon, but 82 Sqn. was subsequently recalled to Watton to arm the aircraft with 500 lb. (227kg.) general purpose bombs with 11-second delay fuses. Nine Blenheims were required to be at two hours readiness on 6 September. At 06.53 82 Sqn. was briefed and scattered, first to Wyton and then to Netheravon.

Mr. K. E. York was a young 19-year-old armourer on 21 Sqn. at the outbreak of war. He and his fellow tradesmen were ordered to arm the Blenheims in preparation for operations. Bombs were loaded, the .303 in. Browning in the port wing was loaded with live ammunition, and seventeen pans of ammunition for the turret-mounted Vickers 'K' machine-gun were stowed on racks adjacent to the turret. Next day, as no operations materialised, the aircraft were disarmed. Two careless incidents took place. Firstly an armourer inadvertently pressed the firing button on the control column and fired a burst from the wing-mounted Browning towards Griston village, across the airfield. Luckily no one was hurt though some rounds hit the church tower! Then an electrician accidentally jettisoned the two 500 lb. bombs from an aircraft onto the tarmac, though luckily safety devices prevented a disaster. This armourer also recalls that most of the missions carried out during the next few months were reconnaissance sorties. Some of his time was also spent in trying to fit extra guns to the Blenheims.

The British Expeditionary Force in France was supported by two main air formations, the RAF Component (BEF) and the Advanced Air Striking Force. It was intended that the latter formation should consist of two echelons, one consisting of Battles of 1 Group and the second of Blenheims of 2 Group. This second echelon would comprise four Blenheim Wings, 79, 81, 82 and 83 — eight squadrons in all

Blenheim IV L8740 of 21 Sqn., carrying code YH, was destroyed by fire when it crash-landed after an engine cut on take-off from Watton on 6 April 1940. [P. H. T. Green collection]

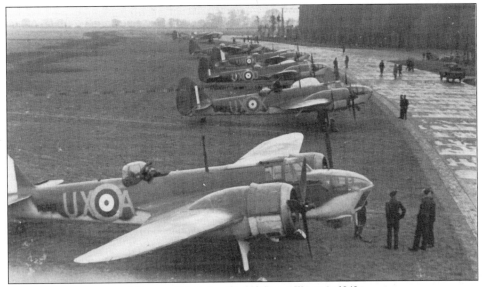

A line-up of Blenheims IV of 82 Sqn. at Watton in 1940.

including both Watton-based units. AASF was to carry out bombing missions into Germany, in particular the industrial areas of the Ruhr.

Due to the lack of airfield facilities and accommodation in France for the Blenheims this plan did not materialise, the squadrons remaining in East Anglia, the intention being to re-equip some of the Battle squadrons with Blenheims. In December 1939 two Battle units did return to the UK to be replaced by the Blenheim IVs of 114 and 139 Sqns. This was abandoned later and only two Blenheim squadrons were retained in the AASF.

During September and October 82 and 105 Sqns. both attacked German gun positions and Channel ports and made night raids on airfields.

Ranges at Otmoor were used for bombing practice and at Cleave for gunnery, and it was at the latter that the first training fatality from Watton occurred. Blenheim IV P4853 of 82 Sqn. crashed on 10 September 1939, seriously injuring the pilot, Sgt. J. McLaughlin, who died in hospital the next day, but the two injured air gunners survived. The 'scatter' plan, while giving protection to squadrons, created logistical

problems, as the aircraft still had to return to base for arming and briefing of crews.

2 Group was standing by from 11 to 16 September, as the German Navy was expected to interfere with Royal Navy minelaying operations in the Straits of Dover. Both Watton squadrons were placed at readiness for this eventuality. The tasks allotted to 2 Group by Bomber Command were reconnaissance and operations against the German Navy, reconnaissance of Luftwaffe airfields in west and north-west Germany and of communications targets. On 13 and 14 September both squadrons were at readiness, and soon two Blenheims of 82 Sqn. were detailed for a photo-reconnaissance mission. Blenheim P4862, flown by Fg. Off. McConnell and crew, photographed Oldenburg and Delmonhurst airfields, while Fg. Off. Hull in P4863 carried out a five-hour sortie photographing Fassberg, Midlum, Luneburg, Stade and Wenzedorf airfields. Both aircraft returned safely.

Similar flights were made on 27 September involving three aircraft from 82 Sqn. and two from 21 Sqn., some of which landed in France to refuel in order to extend the range of their operations. During the operation Plt. Off. Douglas and crew of 82 Sqn. had their first brush with the enemy. Descending below cloud in unfavourable weather, they managed to take accurate photographs from a height of 2000-4000 feet, in the course of which they encountered heavy AA fire over Wunstorf, at one point flying beneath two He.111s which were attempting to land. Cpl Richards opened fire on both but failed to see the result. This operation was flown in conjunction with other 2 Group squadrons, the object being to obtain photographs of twenty-eight Luftwaffe airfields. The future role for 2 Group squadrons during the expected German invasion of the Low Countries and France was tactical support for our armies. Methods of attacking mechanised columns were practiced, interspersed with regular sweeps of the North Sea to look for targets of opportunity, involving flying parallel tracks spaced eight miles (nearly 13 km.) apart.

Two incidents that took place at Watton in the early war years which were recorded by Wg. Cdr. Meston gave rise to suspicion that spies were active there. He recalls that *"The first incident related to the breakout of the German fleet from Kiel. Just after sailing it was sighted but made the correct Royal Naval recognition signals and was allowed to proceed. By the time the error was discovered the German fleet had long gone. At this time I was squadron adjutant and held the Secret Document Register and one of the keys to the safe. One day, having nothing better to do, I decided to do the periodic document check. The Naval Recognition book was missing, which ran for many months ahead, was missing. I assumed the CO of 21 Sqn. (Sqn. Ldr. L.T. Keens) had taken it, and decided to check as he had the only other safe key. He confirmed that he did not have the codes and I was informed that I could be facing a court martial. The Code and Cyphers office at the Air Ministry was phoned and the answer came back that I had never held the document. I was convinced that the book was in the safe and even could describe its contents. It is for conjecture that the book* was involved in the escape of the German fleet and it later transpired that there had been spies at Watton and as my keys were often left on my dressing table they could easily have been duplicated".

"The second incident occured later and may well have had an even greater impact on events. By this time I was a Flight Commander and my best friend Flt. Lt. David Watson one day asked me if I had noticed anything unusual about the country-side. I authorised a flight and we took off to investigate. After about 20 minutes David asked if I could see anything abnormal. I replied that I couldn't. I still remember his reply "Look at the bloody lime heaps" and then it came into focus. The heaps were in straight lines across country complete with arrows. We followed the lines but couldn't make sense of them. We reported this to our squadron CO and eventually it reached the Station Commander, Gp. Capt .Vincent, who chided the CO for listening to two young pilots who had let their imagination run riot. Nevertheless, he took a look himself and informed higher authority. Next day the place was swarming with MI5 and we were told to shut up and not mention this to anyone. About a year later we learned, quite by accident, that the lime heaps were markers for the German airborne invasion of the UK and that in addition there were prepared airfields with filled-in ditches and fold- down hedges".

During the early weeks of September Wg. Cdr. Basil Embry arrived at Watton to report to Gp. Capt. Vincent. Having previously held a staff appointment at the Air Ministry, he was anxious for action and had pressed to be allowed to command a squadron. As a result he was given the command of 21 Sqn. at Watton. After being introduced to aircrews and squadron NCOs later that day he was ordered to 2 Group at Huntingdon for an interview with the Group Commander, AVM Maclean, who told him that he was to be transferred as CO of 107 Sqn. at Wattisham.

A newly promoted Wg. Cdr.took over as CO of 82 Sqn. on 4 December 1939. He was Percy Ronald Gardner Bernard, the 5th

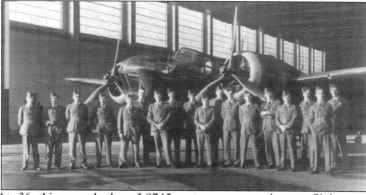

Pilots of 21 Sqn. pose in front of a hangared Blenheim in 1940, the CO, Sqn.Ldr. L. T. Keens, seventh from the left.
[Wg. Cdr. P. Meston]

Earl of Bandon. At 36 this unorthodox Irishman had applied for command of a fighter squadron, but being pronounced too old he was posted to Blenheims. His charm and sense of fun endeared him to his officers and men alike, though his superiors were often shocked by his antics. One of 82 Sqn.'s groundcrew recalls Watton under thick snow. As soon as they were dismissed from their pay parade 'Paddy' Bandon led them on a snowball raid on 21 Sqn. members who were still on parade! Max Hastings, in his book 'Bomber Command', describes an incident when a pilot failed to lower his wheels when landing. Put on open arrest by the enraged Station Commander, he and another officer were summoned to appear before the AOC. 'Paddy' Bandon drove them over to Huntingdon himself and while the AOC was delivering his reprimand he stood behind his senior officer, making faces at the hapless pair in the hope of reducing them to hysterics!

First casualties

On 10 January 1940 Wg. Cdr. the Earl of Bandon led 82 Sqn. on a North Sea sweep. Both squadrons were similarly tasked three days later, but in the latter half of January heavy snow resulted in little flying from Watton, which was under a foot of snow with drifts of four feet. A makeshift runway was constructed by shifting some snow and compressing the rest with rollers. When operations were flown severe icing hampered anti-shipping missions. On 14 February Plt. Off. Stapledon in Blenheim IV

L8745 was on a reconnaissance flight over Borkum and Nordeney when the aircraft iced up and the radio aerial broke under the weight of accumulated ice. Unable to make radio contact with base, the pilot found that his fuel state had become low while he searched for an airfield on which to land. Stapledon ordered his observer and gunner to abandon the aircraft but when he came to leave himself he found that the aircraft went out of control. Deciding to stay with it, he eventually sighted Tangmere and landed safely.

A few weeks later, on 6 February, Sgt. Tice of 21 Sqn. took off in Blenheim L8759 at 05.55 to attempt to obtain information on German warships near Heligoland and Borkum. This aircraft failed to return and was later reported by the German High Command as having been shot down. This was the first Blenheim of 21 Sqn. to be lost by enemy action and also the first from Watton.

The first dusk reconnaissance was flown on 21 February by two Blenheims, the target being Heligoland. To help returning crews to locate Watton, two searchlights were arranged to intersect over the airfield and a further searchlight situated to the east swept the sky to point a finger of light towards the base. On 27 February two from 82 Sqn. took off at 12.53, their task a reconnaissance of Heligoland, the Elbe and Wilhelmshaven. Fg. Off. Blake and crew in Blenheim Z4842 did not return, the first aircraft lost in action by 82 Sqn.

During March and April the Watton

A Ford van, usually referred to as a 'NAAFI wagon' but in this case donated by the people of Uganda to the people of Britain and operated by the Church Army. This picture was taken at Watton's satellite airfield, Bodney, with a Blenheim IV in the background. Ground-crew airmen are enjoying 'char and wads', and on the serving-hatch Craven A and other 'fags' are on sale. [P. Lincoln]

squadrons were given the task of attacking German naval and merchant shipping, much of which was now strongly defended by flak-ships. Nine Blenheims took off on 11 March from Bodney, Watton's newly-opened satellite airfield, on a sortie off the Danish coast. One section found and attacked a group of flak ships and Blenheim P8867, flown by Fg. Off. Harries, was shot down, all three crew being killed on this operation.

Sub sunk!
Sqn. Ldr. Miles Delap was flying on reconnaissance between the Frisian Islands and Heligoland when he sighted enemy submarine U-31 on the surface. He immediately attacked, scoring two hits, one in front of the conning tower. The submarine disappeared in a swirl of water and a large black oil slick was observed, indicating a kill. For this action Sqn. Ldr. Delap was awarded the DFC on 16 March. Since his attack was made at a very low level his aircraft suffered some blast damage, but he managed to bring it back safely. 'Paddy' Delap was at the time a trusted flight commander on 82 Sqn. under Wg. Cdr. the Earl of Bandon.

During the final weeks of March an attempt to attack a German cruiser and escort of four destroyers was unsuccessful. Several sorties were flown alternately by 21 and 82 Sqns., but heavy rain hampered the search. Sqn. Ldr. Pryde crashed while taking off on one of these operations but he and his crew escaped injury.

Between 3 and 8 April 1940 the German invasion of Norway began and a large number of warships and transports left the northern ports of Germany, including the battleships Scharnhorst and Gneisenau. Watton squadrons were again engaged in reconnaissance but bad weather hampered operations. The enemy task force was sighted by other 2 Group Blenheims but a failure in radio communications failed to alert other forces in a follow-up attack.

On 6 April Blenheim IV L8740, flown by Plt. Off. Stapledon, took off from Watton at 04.00 on an anti-submarine patrol but hit a tree and crashed in flames a few miles from the airfield, killing himself and his crew. Two days later an 82 Sqn. Blenheim on a training flight crashed near Swaffham, killing three, but the pilot survived by baling out.

21 and No.82 Sqns. were about to enter a phase of the war where their role in support of our Army in France would result in tragic losses and cause the AOC-in-C Bomber Command, Sir Charles Portal, to question the wisdom *"...of using aircraft as artillery"*, as he aptly put it.

Blitzkreig
10 May 1940 saw the start of the long-expected German invasion of the Low Countries. Squadrons of 2 Group placed at the disposal of the AOC of the Advanced Air Striking Force to give tactical support to the British Expeditionary Force were ordered to reconnoitre advancing enemy columns and attack them. Attempts to stem the enemy

advance over the bridges on the Meuse resulted in heavy losses of aircraft.

On 12 May 82 Sqn. took off to bomb the road alongside the Albert Canal, all aircraft returning safely. Both Watton squadrons were in action on 14 May, 21 Sqn. operating from the satellite, Bodney. Three Blenheims were lost that day operating over Sedan. Plt. Off. R. G. Gilmore in Blenheim L8742 was shot down by fighters and all his crew were killed. Sgt. J. J. Outhwaite and crew in Blenheim L8738 were shot up while attacking enemy troops. A third aircraft, P6890, flown by Fg. Off. J. G. Sarll, was damaged but reached base, where it crash-landed. The only casualty was the wireless operator/air gunner, AC1 L. Lightfoot ,who was wounded in the shoulder by an explosive bullet. At this time air gunners and wireless operators held only aircraftman rank; it was only later in 1940 that for various reasons the rank of Sergeant was established as the minimum aircrew status.

Next day Wg. Cmdr. the Earl of Bandon led twelve Blenheims of 82 Sqn. in an attack on enemy troop concentrations between Mezieres anf Fume, all aircraft returning safely. On 16 May the German Army broke through on a wide front near Gembloux in Belgium. At 04.50 on 17 May twelve Blenheims took off from Watton led by Sqn. Ldr. Delap to attack an enemy column near Gembloux, but this was to prove one of the most tragic days in the history of 82 Sqn. The planned escort of Hurricanes did not materialise and the Germans had moved many anti-aircraft guns in anticipation of an attack. Flying in close formation in two boxes of six aircraft to give maximum defensive cover against fighters, the Blenheims came under intense AA fire near the target area. The first Blenheim to fall was L8830, flown by Fg. Off. R. J. McConnell, which was hit by flak and abandoned. He and his gunner were taken prisoner, but his observer evaded capture and returned to Watton. Under intense AA fire, the formation split up, whereupon the flak ceased and they were set upon by Bf.109 fighters. Within moments

the squadron had been annihilated. Sqn. Ldr. Delap's aircraft was set on fire and both he and his observer, Sgt. P. F. Wyness, baled out ,the third member of his crew, Plt. Off. F. C. Jackson, being killed. One aircraft, though badly shot up, survived to return to base.

In his prize-winning book 'Bomber Command', Max Hastings described the scene at Watton on that fateful day. At 08.20, the handful of aircrew who had not flown and ground crews waiting for the return of their charges wandered out into the sunlight and heard a distant aircraft. As the Blenheim approached they could detect the erratic beat of its single remaining engine. A red Verey light lanced into the sky from the cockpit, and the ambulance and fire tenders bumped hastily across the grass towards the runway. The aircraft wobbled down, bounced, and coasted along the ground until the propellor abruptly stopped. Sgt. Morrison, the pilot, climbed stiffly down from the hatch with his observer, Sgt, Corbutt and Wop/AG LAC Humphreys and sank onto the grass. *"Where's everbody else, Morrison?"* asked Paddy Bandon. Of the thirty-six aircrew who took part in that operation twenty-two were killed and three were taken prisoner. The remainder, including two who evaded capture, returned to their unit .

That same day an order came from 2 Group to disband 82 Sqn., but this was so strongly resisted by 'Paddy' Bandon that after a struggle the order was rescinded. Such was his determination to rebuild his shattered squadron that just three days later he led an attack by 82 and 21 Sqns. against Germans advancing towards Boulogne. Both squadrons continued attempting to delay the enemy advance, in particular to assist the evacuation of the BEF from Dunkirk. On 3 June Watton aircraft were ordered to attack gun batteries, enabling the last remnants of the BEF to be lifted from the beaches.

Despite this evacuation, some 140,000 British troops were still in France after Dunkirk and as they were under increasing pressure, 2 Group squadrons were detailed to provide support. Both 82 and 21 Sqns. were engaged in such operations during the first weeks of June in support of the 51st. Highland Division and the French forces until 22 June, when the French accepted an Armistice. In addition to close support to the Army during this period airfields in France occupied by the Luftwaffe were attacked, operations which were to become a feature of the Watton squadrons' activities.

On 24 June 1940 21 Sqn. moved to Lossiemouth in order to counter any invasion attempt from Norway by bombing airfields and assembly areas. 82 Sqn. was joined at Watton by 105 Sqn., the remnants of which were recovering from their mauling in France. 105 Sqn carried out its first mission on 10 August, the target being Schiphol airfield in Holland. It was on an attack on the Luftwaffe occupied airfield of Aalborg in Denmark that 82 Sqn. was to suffer its second great loss.

Aalborg, 13 August 1940

The operations record book for 82 Sqn. states that twelve aircraft set out to bomb Aalborg aerodrome in formation, at over 20,000 feet altitude if possible. 'A' Flt. took off from Watton and 'B' Flt. from its satellite airfield, Bodney, formated in four stacked vics of three aircraft and flew across the North Sea towards Denmark. Shortly before reaching the Danish coast, Sgt. Baron in Blenheim R3195 broke away from the formation due to a serious fuel shortage. He was subsequently court-martialled but acquited. By this time the remainder of the squadron had, by a navigational error, crossed the Danish coast farther south than intended and at high level had given early warning to German radar operators of an impending attack. Just twenty miles from Aalborg the first Bf.109s attacked. Most of the Blenheims of 'A' Flt. managed to reach the target and drop their bombs but as they reached the coast outbound they were all shot down. First to fall to the Bf.109s was Blenheim R3904, the pilot, Plt. Off. Newland, being the only survivor. Then Sqn. Ldr. Jones in T1827 was shot down and his observer and gunner were killed. Next Flt. Lt. Ellen in R3802 fell victim to the fighters, followed by the squadron CO, Wg. Cdr. E. de Virac Lart, who was leading 'A' Flt. in Blenheim T1934. He and both his

The crews of 'A' Flt. 82 Sqn., at Watton in 1940. [S. Connoly]

crew were killed. Finally Sgt. Oates in T1889 crashed west of Aalborg, sustaining a fractured skull, a broken back and paralysed legs. His observer suffered leg injuries, the WOp/AG escaping uninjured. After hospital treatment the two injured crew and gunner Sgt. Graham became prisoners of war.

'B' Flt. arrived over Aalborg three minutes later to meet an intense flak barrage, the German gunners having established the range. Sqn. Ldr. Wardell led this formation in R3829, which was hit and set on fire. He managed to bale out but his crew were not so fortunate. One attempted to escape but his chute caught on the aircraft and he was dragged to his death. The remaining four Blenheims also fell victim to anti-aircraft guns, R3821 crashing on Aalborg airfield, killing Plt .Off. Hale and his crew.

Twenty aircrew of 82 Sqn. died on this operation and thirteen were taken prisoner. Sgt. Bill Magrath, observer in R2772, was badly injured when the aircraft ditched. After medical treatment by the Germans he was transferred to a PoW camp near Rouen, from which he escaped, crossing the Pyrenees and returning to England, to be awarded the Military Medal. On 16 August 1940 the thirteen dead were buried in Vadum cemetery with full military honours.

Wg. Cdr. Lart's death resulted in Wg. Cdr. J. C. McDonald assuming command of 82 Sqn., and after the Aalborg disaster new tactics were adopted and operating without escort or cloud cover was abandoned. The Battle of Britain was at its height in August and 2 Group operations were designed to counter any invasion plans by attacking barge concentrations and disrupting Luftwaffe attacks by striking at their airfields. In addition, when cloud cover permitted, they raided targets deep in Germany.

As the threat of invasion diminished when Hitler transferred his attention to Russia, 21 Sqn, returned to Watton on 29 October 1940 and 105 Sqn. moved to Swanton Morley two days later.

On the night of 11 November 82 Sqn. sent twelve Blenheims to Hamm, Soest, Osnabruck and Le Havre. During the return flight two aircraft ditched due to lack of fuel, one going down off Harwich and the other off Flamborough Head. Without adequate navigation aids many pilots found great difficulty in finding, let alone bombing, their targets. As an example, on 3 December in a night operation mounted by 82 Sqn. only one aircraft attacked its objective and bad weather at base caused most of the force to divert on their return, in some cases with fatal consequences. Only four aircraft landed safely and only one reached its base.

In the early months of 1941 intruder aircraft of the Luftwaffe were active over RAF airfields in East Anglia. One such attack was carried out on 18 January by fifteen Dorniers of 11/KG3 based at Antwerp. West Raynham was attacked and then Watton, where the NAAFI and married quarters were damaged.

On 10 February Blenheims of 21 Sqn. were part of a force of over two hundred bombers in an attack on Hanover and U-boat component factories. A Blenheim flown by Sqn. Ldr. Sabine was attacked by a Ju.88C flown by Oblt. Semrauz, one of ten aircraft of 1/NJG2 based at Gilze Rijen. The Blenheim crash-landed at Bodney and its crew escaped, but another 21 Sqn. Blenheim was not so lucky. Z5877, flown by Sgt. Chattaway, was attacked as he circled Bodney. He was killed, his observer, Plt Off Cherval died of his wounds and the gunner, Sgt Burch, was wounded in the leg but survived.

Operating in the early morning after attacking Mildenhall, East Wretham and Honington on 18 February, a He.111 of 4/KG53 set course for Watton, where it was brought down by parachute cable shells, one jamming its controls and forcing it to crash-land almost intact at Ovington, some four miles (6.5km.) from Watton, at 07.55. The crew of five survived and were taken prisoner. Swastika and black cross markings normally displayed had been blacked out and a backward-firing gun had been fitted in the tail cone.

In March, as an invasion seemed unlikely, the immediate priority was to ease the mounting shipping losses. Churchill then issued a directive that Bomber Command was to concentrate on naval targets and also assist in the sea blockade of Germany. Thus the two Watton squadrons, 21 and 82, were tasked in the anti-shipping role. This proved to be an extremely hazardous type of operation, as the Blenheims often attacked at very low level and German shipping was heavily defended by flak ships capable of putting up a murderous barrage. 82 Sqn. was in action in March, by which time it had a new CO to replace Wg. Cdr. McDonald. He was a New Zealander, Wg. Cdr. Sam Elworthy, who in later years became MRAF Lord Elworthy, Chief of Defence Staff from 1967 to 1971. On 31 March he led the squadron in an attack on six ships off Le Havre, setting a tanker on fire with a direct hit despite heavy flak. Returning from an attack near Flushing, Elworthy escaped from two Bf.109s, although his gunner was wounded. For this he was awarded the DSO to add to his DFC and AFC, and his gunner, Sgt. Gayfer, won the DFM.

Another attack on 31 March by 21 Sqn. was on enemy shipping off the Frisian Islands. Eight crews took off from Watton and after shipping strikes were briefed to hit coastal targets. This proved dangerous, as it attracted a great deal of anti-aircraft fire during the low-level attack. and two aircraft failed to return from this operation.

Operation 'Circus'

In January 1941 a new tactic was adopted - using a few bombers as bait to entice Luftwaffe aircraft off the ground so that they could be set upon by a large number of fighters. The first such mission, code-named Operation 'Circus', was mounted by six Blenheims of 114 Sqn. (based at Oulton), escorted by no less than nine fighter squadrons. Poor weather delayed further such operations until the beginning of February. The Watton squadrons, in addition to anti-shipping strikes, were also tasked on 'Circus' operations, 21 Sqn.

flying its first in May and completing nine between 21 June and 2 July. On 31 August four Blenheims of 82 Sqn. joined three of 21 Sqn. on a 'Circus'. The final such operation for both squadrons was on 8 November 1941.

Watton airfield suffered an early morning attack on 12 May 1941 by Ju.88s which had already attacked West Raynham, Marham, Waterbeach, Oakington and Stradishall. In the attack on Watton and Bodney, one Ju.88A was shot down by the 121st Light AA Battery. Three crew members were killed and a fourth taken prisoner.

Cologne Power Stations Raid

Squadrons of 2 Group were soon engaged in low-flying practice on a massive scale for a very special operation which involved penetrating deep into Germany. The targets were the two giant power stations at Knapsack and Quadrath, the combined output of which was 800,000 kilowatts, and the effect of their destruction on German factories would be catastrophic. A complex operation was planned, including diversionary tactics, the use of Whirlwind fighters as long range escorts and Spitfires to cover the withdrawal. 2 Group was to provide fifty-four Blenheims, including nine from 21 Sqn. at Watton and nine from 82 Sqn. at Bodney. In addition, four Flying Fortresses, newly in service with the RAF, would take part. The raid comprised two elements: Force 1, the Watton and Bodney aircraft, briefed to attack Quadrath, took off at 09.50 on 12 August 1941, led by Wg. Cdr. Kercher. One Blenheim of 82 Sqn. was shot down by flak at Strijdens, the crew being killed, but the rest of the force attacked Quadrath and reported that the power station had been set ablaze. 17 Blenheims landed at Watton at 13.21. The larger power station at Knapsack was successfully attacked by Force 2, consisting of Blenheims from 18, 107, 114 and 139 Sqns. 2 Group lost twelve aircraft in this operation, which was not surprising since this was the largest low-level raid and the deepest penetration into Germany to date.

A low level anti-shipping operation was made against Rotterdam on 28 August. Watton provided six Blenheims from 2I Sqn. and Swanton Morley and Wattisham each supplied six, while two Spitfire squadrons from Coltishall were responsible for long range escort duties. Heavy losses were sustained by the bombers from low-flying accidents and fighter activity. Twelve aircraft failed to return, one Bf.109 from 6/NG53 accounting for two Blenheims of 21 Sqn. Hits were obtained by 21Sqn. on two ships and on the docks.

Arrival of the Flying Fortress

90 Sqn. had been transferred as a front line squadron to become a training unit and later the nucleus of 17 OTU. On 7 May 1941 the squadron was reformed at Watton to be the first squadron to receive the B-17 Flying Fortress from the United States, with Wg. Cdr. J. C.MacDougall DFC from 101 Sqn. at West Raynham in command. First aircraft to arrive was AN521, which landed at Ayr from Gander, Newfoundland after being flown over the Atlantic by Maj. Walshe of the USAAC in 8 hours 26 minutes, the shortest time so far. The first RAF pilot to receive training was Plt. Off. Roake, who subsequently failed an oxygen test at Farnborough. 90 Sqn. was formed from experienced crews from all Groups, with an age limit of 24 years, all of whom had to pass an oxygen test of 4 hours at 35,000 feet. From 8 to 10 May the crews, who came from 35, 51, 77, 102 and 115 Sqns., attended lectures on the new aircraft.

A Boeing expert on the Sperry bomb-sight flew over from the United States to advise crews on its use. Wg. Cdr. MacDougall and Maj. Walshe flew a Flying Fortress to Great Massingham for circuits and landings to determine whether it was a suitable airfield to be used as a base for the new type. From 12 May all flying was carried out at Bodney, but it very soon became clear that this airfield was quite unsuitable for the Fortress. The CO was called to 2 Group headquarters, where it was decided that Great Massingham would make a better base for the Fortresses. On 14 May a B-17 was flown from Bodney to Watton and the AOC 2 Group and Wg. Cdr. Elworthy flew a circuit in the aircraft with Wg. Cdr. MacDougall and were favourably impressed. After further consultation it was decided to move 90 Sqn., and so on 15 May 90 Sqn. left Watton to be based at West Raynham, its aircraft flying from Great Massingham.

The massive (for those days) Fortress I was introduced to the RAF by 90 Sqn. at Watton in May 1941, but moved to West Raynham after one week. This example, AN530 [WP:F], was previously 40-2066 of the USAAC. [P. H. T. Green collection]

Detachments

While retaining Watton as a main base, 82 and 21 Sqns. frequently detached temporarily to other airfields as required to meet operational contingencies. A second detachment began operations at Lossiemouth in May 1941, returning to Watton in June. Lossiemouth gave the Blenheims a considerable reduction in transit time when engaged on anti-shipping operations off Norway and north-west Germany. On 26 April 1941 six crews from 21 Sqn. were moved to Luqa in Malta as a trial to test the effectiveness and feasability of operating against Axis shipping sailing between Europe and North Africa in supplying Rommel's forces. It was planned that if this was successful squadrons would be tropicalised at Watton and sent to Malta for periods of five weeks. The small element of 21 Sqn. returned to Watton before being based at Manston for a week. In September they went for another short stay at Lossiemouth. Finally the whole squadron was posted to Malta, arriving at the end of December 1941 to operate against Axis ships in the Mediterranean and various land targets in North Africa. It remained in Malta until disbanded in March 1942 but reformed immediately at Bodney.

82 Sqn. was detached to Lossiemouth in April 1941 to carry out anti-shipping strikes off Norway before returning to Bodney on 3 May 1941, when Wg. Cdr. L. V. E. Atkinson assumed command. Six Blenheims were ordered to Luqa on 19 May and shortly afterwards two were lost on operations. The remainder of 82 Sqn. began to move to Malta on 4 June and completed the move a week later. On 22 June six aircraft attacked an Axis convoy off Lampedusa and Sqn. Ldr. Harrison Broadley in Z6122 was hit by flak, disabling both engines and forcing him to ditch. He and his crew were picked up and hecame prisoners. For pressing home his attack after being hit he was awarded the DFC.

Ports also came in for the attention of the squadron's Blenheims but the attrition rate soon caused the survivors to be recalled to Bodney to rebuild. After a short period of rehabilitation and re-equipping 82 Sqn. recommenced operations, which consisted of shipping strikes, 'Circus' operations and intruder raids against enemy-occupied airfields. Wg. Cdr. J. McMichael took command in February 1942 and the squadron moved to the Far East at the end of March.

At some time during 1941 or 1942, Watton's original 'Fort' type control tower was replaced by a wartime utility building type 12779/41, modified to have smaller windows, to provide much more space for the additional staff needed under wartime conditions.

Into a Training Role

To train pilots in blind landing procedures, 1505 Beam Approach Training (BAT) Flight, equipped with Blenheims, moved from Horsham St. Faith to Watton on 20 December 1941. A radio beam aligned with the runway was followed by the trainees, who listened to audible notes in their headsets. A steady note indicated that they were on the beam, while diversion from it was indicated by dots on one side and dashes the other. Inner and outer marker beacons gave audible signals when they were overflown, as an indication of the distance from touchdown. This unit returned to Horsham St. Faith on 1 September 1942.

17 (Pilot) Advanced Flying Unit (PAFU) was formed at Watton on 19 January 1942 under Sqn. Ldr. B. P. King, and the first Miles Masters Mk.II began to arrive. PAFUs were established to give pilots experience in aircraft with a performance approaching that of the operational type they were destined for, and also to familiarise them with flying in UK weather conditions, as many had trained in the United States and the Commonwealth in near-perfect weather conditions. Watton's medical officer soon noted that an epidemic of colds and sinusitis was evident amongst many trainees, thought to be because colonial pilots had contracted colds on arriving in England and had been unable to

WATTON

shake them off.

On 2 February 1942 forty-eight pupil pilots were posted in to form No.1 Course, and flying cornmenced on 8 February. Two fatal accidents occured during the month, both pilots being members of the Royal New Zealand Air Force, Sgts. B. S. Wilder and A Holmes, the latter losing his life during a night-flying exercise. Both were buried in Watton churchyard.

Course sizes increased to satisfy the requirement for pilots and No.7 Course comprised one hundred and sixteen pupils. This so stretched accommodation at Watton

that twenty bell tents were erected on the sports field next to the Sergeants' Mess. Many officers were housed at Clermont Hall, which also served as the Officers' Mess for 21 Sqn.

On 10 April 1942 Lancaster ED724 of Elsham Wolds-based 103 Sqn. crash-landed at Bodney after being badly shot up over Germany. The tail gunner was dead, the rear turret completely burnt out. The mid-upper gunner had numerous shrapnel wounds in the arm and leg and the flight engineer burns to his hands, but the rest of the crew were uninjured.

During a visit to Watton, Air Cmdre. HRH the Duke of Kent is seen about to climb into a requisitioned Humber staff car of 2 group, Bomber Command.[P. Lincoln].

Sqn. Ldr. King was promoted to Wg. Cdr. and on 21 July Air Cdre. HRH the Duke of Kent visited Watton and made a tour of No.17 (P) AFU. A week later Wg. Cdr. King was invested with the AFC at Buckingham Palace by King George VI.

Flying training at Watton continued, but not without accidents, many of them fatal. Two Masters collided during formation practice on 9 November, the two Sergeant pilots luckily escaping by parachute. Also in November, a fatal crash involving two Masters resulted in the deaths of Sgts. Hoggin and Hibbert, and there were two more mishaps in December. On the 6th Master II AZ589 crashed near Kings Lynn, killing Sgt. N. Mortimere and seriously injuring Sgt. E. T. Smith. Next day Sgt. F. R. Huntsinger died in Rauceby Hospital from injuries received in a crash on 30 November. On 3 January 1943 Sgts. Rose and Govett were killed when Master II DL952 crashed. When Master II DL800 crashed at Fulbourn in Cambridgeshire on 20 January both pupils, Sgts. R. Fahey and R. Sward, were killed. Flt. Sgt. N. G. Clark RNZAF was killed while night flying solo in Master II DM216 when its engine cut during an overshoot at Bodney on 25 February 1943. Ground accidents were rarer, but on 24 March, when a Master taxied into a petrol bowser, the pilot was unhurt but the bowser driver, Cpl. Burrows, was hit by the propellor and died from head injuries.

It was then decided to move 17 (P) AFU out of the East Anglian operational area to allow Watton to revert to operational use. The airfield chosen as 17 (P) AFU's new base was Calveley, near Wrexham, and on 3 May 1943 twelve Masters were flown there, followed on 21 May by forty-three more, sixteen of them piloted by instructors and the remainder by advanced pupils.

Arrival of the US 8th Air Force

The first Americans arrived at Watton on 23 July 1943 to open the 3rd Strategic Air Depot (SAD) of the US Eighth Air Force, referred to as Neaton (Station 505). Air Depots carried out repairs and modifications to aircraft and supplied spares to Bomb Groups of the USAAF. In addition the 3rd SAD had the task of salvaging any B-24s that crashed or force-landed in the UK, obtaining any useful parts, or if the aircraft was repairable flying it or transporting it by road back to Watton . 3rd SAD was responsible in this role for all aircraft in the 2nd Air Division, which in effect was all B-24 aircraft operating in the European theatre. Two of the type 'C' hangars were handed over as engineering sections.

In August 1943 Watton was becoming very overcrowded, the RAF still being present. It was then decided that the Station would be taken over wholly by the Americans, the official transfer was effected on 4 October, and by November the RAF had left. In preparation for the arrival of flying units the 3rd SAD moved to the south site of the airfield, near Griston village.

Secret Operations

The first USAAF flying units arrived from the 801st Bombardment Group at Alconbury on 27 February 1944, and RAF Watton became Station 376. Engaged on highly secret missions known as 'Carpetbagger' operations, ther role of the 801st was to drop agents of the Office of Strategic Services (OSS) into enemy-occupied territories, with supplies and pro-

Carpetbagger B-24D 42-63775 of the 856th BS, 801st BG. [via H. Friedman]

WATTON

paganda leaflets to resistance units and patriots. Regular missions were flown over France, Belgium, Holland, Denmark and Scandanavia at night in adverse weather conditions and with strong opposition from enemy ground forces The 801st BG is known to have operated at least one 'Carpetbagger' squadron, the 406th BS, from Watton for approximately two months. Aircraft used were B-24s specially modified for this cloak- and-dagger role and painted black. Ball turrets and bomb racks were removed and a cargo hatch installed. The 801st BG contained two other squadrons, the 856th and 858th BS, and it would appear they also operated from Watton as 'Carpetbaggers'. By May 1944 four squadrons with a total of forty B-24s were engaged on these secret missions and between January and May twenty-five were lost. Records state that the 406th BS moved from Watton in March 1944 though one source indicates that 'Carpetbagger' missions were flown from Watton until September. Operations then moved to the headquarters at Harrington, conveniently close to RAF Tempsford, from where similar flights were undertaken for the Special Operations Executive (SOE).

Weather Reconnaissance
On 22 April 1944 the 802nd Reconnaissance Group (Provisional) was established at Watton with its component squadrons, the 652nd BS (Heavy), the 653rd BS (Light) and the 654th BS (Special). 652nd BS was tasked with obtaining meteorological data over the Atlantic and adjacent waters, weather information being vital in planning combat missions, using B-

24s and B-17Gs. The 653rd BS operated B-24s, B-17Gs and Mosquitos Mk.XVI, engaged chiefly in weather flights over the continent and later weather scouting missions ahead of bomber formations and visual observation of target strikes. The 654th BS flew rnainly day and night photo-reconnaissance sorties and also later dropped radar reflecting aluminium 'chaff' to screen the bombers from enemy radar operators. Mosquito pilots in these units were former P-38 pilots from the 50th Fighter Squadron. The 654th BS is also recorded as operating the B-26 and the P-38.

Until July 1944 Watton's main runway was of steel matting, but that month, significantly for Watton's long-term future, the 899th Engineer Bn. of the US Army began the construction of a single concrete runway, perimeter track and fifty-three hardstandings, necessitating the closure of two roads. The 3rd SAD was provided with 24 loop-type hardstandings and three grouped T2 hangars.

On 9 August 1944 the 802nd Reconaissance Group was redesignated as the 25th Bombardment Group (Recon.), (part of the 325th Photo Wing), with Lt. Col. Joseph A. Stenglein as its CO until 23 September, when Col. Leon W. Gray took over. By September sixteen Mosquitos had been lost and the Air Ministry was asked to supply replacements, but luckily by early 1945 losses had considerably reduced and deliveries were halted. The war in Europe came to a close and in July 1945 the 652nd BS moved to Alconbury before returning to the United States in December. The 653rd BS moved to Chalgrove before joining the 652nd at Camp Kilmer, New Jersey in

Mosquito NS538 was equipped with H2S radar installed in abulbous nose. It is seen here in the colours of the 654th BS during start up at Watton in the summer of 1944. [via G. Simons]

December, and after de-activation on 23 July the 654th BS left Watton to return home to Drew Field, Florida in August 1945. Watton was about to be returned to the Royal Air Force.

Radio Warfare Establishment

During the war the success of radio counter-measures in confusing German defences had a considerable effect in reducing bomber losses. Detection of enemy radar and radio devices and developing methods of countering them received increasing resources as the war progressed. The first notable success in the radio war was the detection of the Luftwaffe's blind bombing aid known as 'Knickebein'. This equipment allowed accurate bombing at night using a narrow beam which was received on Lorenz beam equipment modified to give increased sensitivity to enable it to be used at long range. Three Ansons based at Wyton were used to investigate and attempt to detect this beam. The third flight, made by Flt. Lt. H. E. Bufton with special wireless operator Cpl. Mackie, took off from Wyton on the night of 21 June 1940. On return they reported picking up a narrow beam signal on a frequency of 31.5 mHz modulated at 1150 Hz which passed one mile south of Spalding, with dots to the north and dashes to the south. As a result of this evidence, together with intelligence gained from Luftwaffe prisoners and captured equipment, a special unit to counter this scheme was established. This was 80 Wing, the first commanding officer of which was

Wg. Cdr. E. B. Addison, who later as an Air Cmdre. commanded 100 (Bomber Support) Group. 80 Wg. operated ground-based equipment which transmitted dashes on the 'Knickebein' frequencies to confuse German pilots attempting to fly the beam. 100 Group was formed on 23 November 1943 to provide radio countermeasures, its importance evident from the fact that it occupied some ten airfields in Norfolk between 1943 and 1945. Two units in 100 Group which were to be based at Watton immediately after the war were 192 and 199 Sqns. 192 Sqn., the first to join 100 Group, was formed from 1474 Flight, which in turn had evolved from 'A' Flight of 109 Sqn., which at the time was closely involved in the development of the RAF's own blind bombing device, 'Oboe'.

Above: Doing her bit as part of the entertainments circuit was Marlene Deitrich, seen here at Watton with the CO of the 25th BG, Col. Leon Gray. [P. Lincoln]

Left: Gen. James Doolittle (centre) visited the 25th Bomb Group (Reconnaissance) at Watton and is seen here standing in front of a Mosquito of that unit. nThe tall officer behind his right shoulder is thought to have been Col. Elliott Roosevelt, son of the President of the United States. [P. Lincoln]

WATTON

At the end of the war in Europe Watton became the sole base for radio warfare development. Known as the Radio Warfare Establishment, it received a variety of aircraft from different units engaged in electronic intelligence and radio-countermeasures (abbreviated to Elint and RCM). First to move to Watton was 192 Sqn., which arrived on 27 Sept 1945 from Foulsham. Gp. Capt. Jack Short had been a tail gunner with 192 Sqn., flying Wellington Mk.X on 'Elint' operations in 1944. He recalls that at the end of the war he was sent to Watton with an advance party to earmark accommodation and offices prior to the move of the squadron. The move from Nissen-hutted accommodation at Foulsham to the luxury of a permanent station was welcomed by all. 192 Sqn.'s aircraft at this time were Halifax IIIs, Mosquito XVIs, Ansons and Oxfords. 199 Sqn. had flown

Halifaxes and Stirlings as part of 100 Group to jam German radio and radars. Equipped with a radar jammer code-named 'Mandrel' and VHF radio jammers known as 'Airborne Cigar' and 'Jostle',they complemented the intelligence-gathering 192 Sqn. In August 199 Sqn. flew to Foulsham to disband into 192 Sqn. before the final move to Watton. Both squadrons then temporarily lost their identity and became the Radio Warfare Establishment. However, this name was thought to be too self-evident for such a secret unit and it was renamed the Central Signals Establishment under its parent formation, 90 (Signals) Group. Keith Thompson DFC, who had flown Halifaxes on 'Mandrel' jamming operations with 199 Sqn., recalls that between November 1945 and January 1946 they carried out navigation exercises, air-to-sea gunnery and general continuation

At the Battle ofBritain open day held at Watton on 18 September 1948 this Meteor F.4, RA487 [MR:R] was a visitor from 245 Sqn., based at Horsham St. Faith. [Tony Cramp]

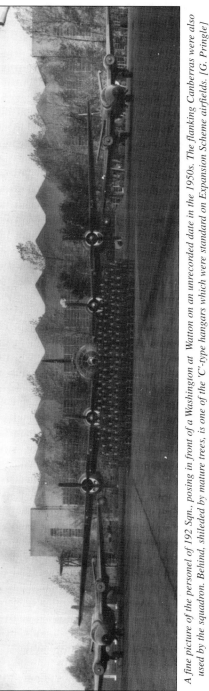

A fine picture of the personel of 192 Sqn., posing in front of a Washington at Watton on an unrecorded date in the 1950s. The flanking Canberras were also used by the squadron. Behind, shileded by mature trees, is one of the 'C'-type hangars which were standard on Expansion Scheme airfields. [G. Pringle]

training. Some conversion to Lancasters by Halifax crews was carried out and also some Fortresses were operated from Watton. It is most probable that these were former 214 Sqn. aircraft used during the war for RCM purposes. Fortress IIs and IIIs of 214 Sqn. had been specially modified with a large bulbous nose to house H2S and with bomb bays sealed to take jamming gear such as 'Mandrel' and 'Jostle'. Another unit at Watton at this time was 527 Sqn., which moved from Digby on 12 November 1945 equipped with the Spitfire Vb, Oxford, Dominie and Wellington X aircraft, only to disband five months later.

One of the most unusual people to have served at RAF Watton was Leo Dalderup, alias LAC George Gallagher, who arrived on 6 June 1949 for a GCA operators' course. A Dutchman, 18-year-old Dalderup had joined the German Army in order to make a military career. He had fought Russians on the Eastern Front and Americans and British on the Western Front before being taken prisoner. After escaping from a PoW camp in northern England, he reached Northern Ireland and then the Irish Republic, where he laid low for six months. He then decided that the only way out of his predicament was to take a very bold decision — to join the Royal Air Force! With assistance from Irish friends he obtained a copy birth certificate in the name of George Vincent Gallagher, a man of about Leo's own age. Armed with this, he reported to the RAF recruiting office in Belfast and was accepted, nobody questioning his slight foreign accent. In February 1948 he began basic training at RAF Cardington, where he had to suppress his previous training and pretend to be a raw recruit. From Cardington he went to Yatesbury and Welford before his eventual posting to Watton.

With the advent of the Cold War it became essential to gain up-to-date intelligence on the military capability and level of technology of the Soviet bloc. In early post war years the Soviet radar defences were rudimentary and largely concentrated on the borders with the west.

Right: Among the several types of aircraft used by 527 Sqn. at Watton was the Anson, here exemplified in September 1953 by TX170, a C.19. [author]

Below: Lincoln II RE359 served with several bomber squadrons before reaching Watton and the Development Sqn. [C. Shutt]

Surface-to-air missiles had not entered service and thus it was possible for 'Elint' aircraft of the Western alliance to fly close to or even over Soviet territory with impunity.

It was against this background that 192 Sqn. was re-established at Watton on 17 July 1951. As its activities in 1943 had included mapping radars in western Europe and the Mediterranean using Wellingtons, Mosquitos and Halifaxes, it had a pedigree in electronic intelligence-gathering and it

was this role it again assumed. Aircraft used initially were the Lincoln B.2 and Mosquito PR.34, until re-equipping in April 1952 with three specially-adapted B-29A Washingtons (WZ966, WZ967 and WZ968). These were joined by Canberra B.2s in January 1953 and Canberra B.6s in July 1954. The Washington, in addition to a usual flight crew, carried a team of special operators trained to search for and measure the parameters of Soviet radio and radar signals. As these radars advanced and

Canberra B.2 WJ603 [K], inscribed 'Royal Air Force No.90 (Signals) Group', served with a number of squadrons, including 98 Sqn. at Watton, although this picture was taken elsewhere. [P. H. T. Green collection]

'Iris III' was a Watton-based Hastings C.2, WJ338, used by Signals Command to monitor air traffic control radio transmissions.

proliferated, with frequencies moving into a wider area of the electromagnetic spectrum, an 'Elint' aircraft with a greater detection capacity became necessary. Thus it was decided to replace the Washingtons, and the aircraft chosen was the Comet 2. Following disasters to. the civil Comets, BOAC had opted for the improved Comet 4. Three Comet 2s surplus to BOAC requirements were ordered and after equipment and racks had been fitted by Marshalls of Cambridge they were completely equipped at Watton. First to arrive at Watton, on 19 April 1957, was Comet XK663 (formerly G-AMXE). The second aircraft, XK659 (G-AMXC), arrived at Watton on 12 July 1957 and joined 192 Sqn. on 14 March 1958, followed by the third Comet XK655 (G-AMXA). The Washingtons were withdrawn from service on 24 March 1958 and on 21 August 1958

192 Sqn. was disbanded, to be immediately reformed as 51 Sqn. Comet XK663 was destroyed by fire in a hangar at Watton on 3 June 1959. Its replacement was Comet 2CR XK695 (ex G-AMXH), which had served with 216 Sqn. at Lyneham as a transport aircraft from 1957 to 1960, surviving two accidents. It finally reached Watton on 8 March 1963, just before 51 Sqn.'s transfer to Bomber Command from Signals Command and its move to Wyton on 31 March.

Watton was responsible for training special operators for both 192 and 51 Sqns., using Varsity aircraft. Other non-'Elint' Comet 2s were used at various times for flight crew continuation training and conversion. These included XK697, XK715 and XK671.

Little detail can be written, for

Mosquito B.35 TK629 of CSE, carrying the unit's code V7:Z, is seen here away from home at Prestwick in January 1951.
[M. C. Gray]

The stocky proportions of a 'Flying Pig' — Varsity T.1 — are seen in this shot of WL685 [S] of Watton-based 116 Sqn.

obvious security reasons, of operations carried out by 192 and 51 Sqns. and those who took part still maintain a strict silence. The importance attached to these covert flights is reflected in the many awards given to squadron aircrew, which included the Air Force Cross, Air Force Medal and Queen's Commendation.

527 Squadron

Well before the outbreak of war in 1939 a chain of early warning radar stations had been installed around the east coast of Britain. The brain child of Robert Watson Watt, the system was known as Radio Direction Finding (RDF). In 1937 twenty stations, known as Chain Home (CH) stations, were approved. These were pulsed radar stations, all synchronised at 25 pulses per second using half the frequency of the electricity supply but differing transmitter frequencies within the 20 Mhz band to avoid mutual interference. With the Ground Controlled Interception (GCI) radars used to control fighters, the role played by these stations in the Battle of Britain is legendary. The ending of the war heralded the start of the Cold War and thus the necessity to refurbish the existing CH stations, which remained in service until

Above and below: Five aircraft of the Lincoln Flt. of 151 Sqn. at Watton. From the left are RF398 (which became 8376M as a ground instructional airframe), RA685, RF505, RF461 and another. All were Mk.II, and none saw further service after the squadron disbanded. [R. Kennett]

An early Valetta C.1 of 115 Sqn., VX542, at Watton during an open day.

being replaced by newer technology in the mid-1950s.

One of Watton's units involved in the calibration of the CH and GCI stations was 527 Squadron. Initially using Lancasters but later converting to the Lincoln, the squadron regularly calibrated all the CH, CHL and GCI radars from Cornwall to the Orkneys. Calibration of GCI stations in Europe also was also one of its responsibilities.

The calibration Lincoln carried a reduced crew of four: pilot, flight engineer, navigator and signaller, the two gunners and radar navigator which were in the usual Lincoln bomber establishment being superfluous in its new role. 527 Sqn. had originally been designated Calibration 'R' Sqn. but was given its number on 1 August 1952, with the motto *"Silently we serve"*.

Calibration flights were long tedious routines often flown at high altitudes on oxygen in less than comfortable conditions. The heating system of the Lincoln was notorious for cold and hot spots, giving unequal degrees of comfort (or discomfort) to the crew. Because of the dispersed locations of the CH stations, crews had frequent detachments away from base, which gave a certain variety to the work.

Lincolns were used at Watton longer than at any other RAF station and WD130, WD141, WD142, WD147, RE291, RE325, SX945 and SX950 were flown by 527 Sqn. at various times. Possibly one of the largest squadrons in the service, 527 Sqn. consisted of three flights, 'A' Flt. with Lincolns, 'B' Flt. with Anson C.19s (later Varsities), and 'C' Flt. with Mosquitoes (later Meteors NF.11 and NF.14).

In 1954 a Meteor NF.14 of 527 Sqn. was tasked to calibrate a GCI station in Germany, with pilot Sgt Don Coleman and navigator Flt. Sgt. Bill Fricker. On completion of the final check run, as was customary, the crew obtained a course to steer for base from the same GCI radar but were accidentally given a reciprocal which, combined with a fuel shortage, resulted in a forced landing in a field the wrong side of the Iron Curtain! After a brief period as uninvited guests of the East Germans, the crew were returned.

On 21 August 1958 527 Sqn. was disbanded, renumbered 245 Sqn. and moved to Tangmere, but on 19 April 1963 it was renumbered 98 Sqn. and returned to Watton equipped with Canberra B.2s. There it remained for the next six years. An experienced Canberra captain, Master Pilot Eric Quinney, who had also flown Canberras and Comets with 51 Sqn., recalls his work. *"The role of 98 Sqn. was basically calibration of UK radar stations from GCA high level search and at all levels in between. It had its exciting bits as well as boring bits. Flying at heights contrary to standard flight patterns in cloud and being informed by your controlling radar station that they had lost you in cloud! Trips were normally of three hours duration, very monotonous."* 98 Sqn. moved from Watton to Cottesmore on 17 April 1969.

WATTON

WH857, a Canberra B.2 of 97 Sqn., seen here on a trip to Malta, was the victim of a stalled approach to Watton on 3 May 1966 and was destroyed by fire. [R. C. B. Ashworth via P. H. T. Green]

116 Squadron

Calibration 'N' Squadron reformed as 116 Sqn. on 1 August 1952 and carried out sight checking of radio and radar navigational aids and landing aids, covering equipment such as HF and VHF direction finding, BABS and Ground Control Approach (GCA) radars. A special Hastings aircraft was also on squadron strength. Known as 'Iris', it was used by the Inspectorate of Radio Services, an organisation established to carry out world-wide tours of inspection, checking on the efficiency, organisation, operation and maintenance of RAF ground-to-air communications. Formed in 1946, IRS originally used a Lancaster, 'Iris 1'. The Inspectorate was disestablished on 17 August 1973, the responsibility for maintaining standards being passed to individual commands. During the period in which it operated, the fact that 'Iris' might be listening in made sure that the highest standards were maintained in the vital area of radio communications.

116 Sqn. also operated Lincolns and Anson C.19s, which were replaced by Varsities. Lincoln serial numbers included RE308, RE311, WD124 and SX956 and Varsities were WL685, WL621 ,WL692 and WJ945.

On 21 August 1958 116 Sqn. became 115 Sqn. and four days later moved to Tangmere with 245 Sqn. Both squadrons returned to Watton five years later, on 1 October 1963, by which time 245 Sqn. had been redesignated 98 Sqn.

It was in 1946 that the Central Signals establishment had been formed but in June 1963 the Station was revived as a seperate entity and remained so until 30 September 1983, when a change in establishment redesignated CSE as a lodger unit upon RAF Watton. In October 1965 Eastern Radar was established and came into operation as a parented unit adjacent to the Station. It was controlled by the Military Air Traffic Organisation and gave radar control and surveillance to all aircraft flying over East Anglia.

Development Squadron.

This unit, formerly known as Research and Development Sqn., became Development Sqn. from October 1956, 'A' Flight with Canberras and 'B' Flight with Lincolns, the latter being the last such aircraft in the RAF. Involved in development of Radar Countermeasures (RCM), it also gave training to defence radar operators, enabling them to recognise and cope with jamming. On 1 January 1962 it became 151 Sqn., which in addition to the Lincoln flew the Hastings, Varsity and Canberra.

To give crews experience in long-range navigation, overseas trips were arranged, which also provided a break from routine. One such trip during the author's service with the squadron had an unexpected sequel. Lincoln SX948, flown by Flt. Lt. Roy Matthews and crew, left Watton on a planned 'navex' to Malta, the next leg to Tripoli (Idris), then to Gibraltar and a final leg to base. On this trip the Lincoln carried as passenger a member of HM Customs, Duggie Haig. Mr Haig was retiring from the service at Kings Lynn and, as one of the

Converted from a B.2 to a T.17, Canberra WJ625, seen here landing at Watton in August 1968, belonged to 360 Sqn. It met its fate as recently as 2 August 1983, when it crashed into the sea off Gibraltar, still in use by 360 Sqn. but from Wyton. [R. A. Walker via P. H. T. Green]

officers often responsible for clearing Watton aircraft following overseas trips, always treated crews extremely fairly. As a gesture of appreciation he was invited on the flight to celebrate his retirement. Taking off from Idris, the Lincoln set course for Gibraltar, extra care being taken to avoid certain prohibited areas set up by the French to prevent gun-running to Arab terrorists active in Morocco. Flying with few radio aids, the Lincoln suddenly found itself accompanied by French Air Force Vampires, the pilots of which gave clear signals that they wanted the Lincoln to follow them. The Lincoln crew complied and eventually landed at Oran, where they found themselves surrounded by armed French troops. Seemingly the flight plan had not reached the French authorities, with the result that the unannounced arrival of the Lincoln in their airspace was mistaken for gun-running. After their credentials had been confirmed the crew were taken to lunch and invited to stay. It so happened that two French aircraft had been diverted to Gibraltar due to weather conditions, and a signal was passed to the French at Oran

which read "You have one of ours, we have two of yours. Game and set to us"!

12 March 1963 saw the final flypast of the Lincolns in RAF service and on 25 May 151 Sqn. was renumbered 97 Sqn., which continued to fly the Canberra, Varsity and Hastings until disbanding on 2 January 1967, 'B' Flt. of the squadron having been absorbed into the newly-formed joint RAF/RN 360 Sqn..

On 30 September 1966 a unique presentation was made to three squadrons at Watton to mark 25 years of service. This was a particularly special event as the officer presenting colours simultaneously to 97, 98 and 115 Sqns. was ACM The Earl of Bandon GBE CB CVO DSO, who had been the CO of 82 Sqn. at Watton in 1940 during one of the most tragic periods in that squadron's history.

The Royal Navy at Watton

751 Sqn. Fleet Air Arm, which had dis-banded at Machrihanish on 31 October 1945, reformed at Watton on 1 March 1947 and operated Oxford, Seafire XV and Anson aircraft as a Radar Trials unit until

Left: 751 Sqn. operated this Sea Mosquito TR.33, TW250, at Watton.

Below:Seen at Abbotsinch in July 1960, Avenger AS 4 XB311 had flown with 751 Sqn at Watton. [both via R. C. Sturtivant]

disbanding again on 30 September 1947.

It next reformed at Watton as a Radio Warfare Unit at the Central Signals Establishment on 3 December 1951, commanded initially by Lt. Cdr. P. Winter DSC and in March 1952 by Lt. Cdr. G. R. Woolston. The squadron was based at Watton for the next six years with frequent detachments to take part in Fleet exercises, at times operating from carriers. It flew a variety of aircraft in the RCM role, including the Mosquito FB.6 and PR.34, Sea Mosquito TR.33, Avenger AS.4, Firefly AS.6, Sea Fury FB.11 and Anson. The squadron moved on 27 September 1957 to Culdrose, where on 1 May 1958 it was renumbered 831 Sqn. and given the title of an Electronic Warfare squadron. Initially 831 Sqn. comprised 'A' Flight with four Grumman Avenger AS.6s and 'B' Flight with four Sea Venom 21.ECMs. The squadron returned to Watton in July 1963 to work more closely with its RAF

counterpart, 98 Sqn., by which time the Avengers had been replaced by Gannet ECM.6s. On 16 May 1966 the squadron was 'paid off' when personnel were transferred to 360 Sqn. of the RAF for joint RAF/RN trials and training in ECM work, but was not disbanded officially until 26 August that year.

360 Squadron

This unique RAF/RN squadron was formed on 1 April 1966 to provide ECM training for all three services. Though manned by mixed RAF and RN air and ground crews, inter-service cooperation was extremely high. The squadron was 25% manned and funded by the Royal Navy and every fourth commanding officer came from that service. Expansion came about on 10 October 1966, when 'B' Flt. of 97 Sqn. was absorbed. The squadron flew a specially modified Canberra B.2, the E.17, crammed with ECM gear and specially designed wingtip pods

Right: In front of the former Officers' Mess stands a memorial to the men of the 25th BG and its subsidiary units

Below: The front entrance to the former Officers' Mess, seen in August 1996, with the memorial to the 25th BG in the foreground. The bent propeller was recovered from Blenheim R3800 of 82 Sqn., which was shot down over Aalborg, Denmark, on 13 August 1940.[author]

for dispensing 'Window'. Canberras operated by 360 Sqn. carried pilot, navigator and air electronics officer (or elecronic warfare officer), who was responsible for operating all the ECM gear. A similar unit, 361 Sqn., had a brief life at Watton, forming on 2 January 1967 under the control of 360 Sqn. but disbanding into it on 14 July that year.

360 Sqn. left Watton for Cottesmore on 21 April 1969, the year in which all three flying units left Watton for Cottesmore. However, this was not the end of RAF tenure of the airfield, as prominent on the western edge of the station in the mid 1960s was a large Type 82 radar, controlling aircraft over East Anglia, which became Eastern Radar until closing in 1988. Between January 1959 and June 1963 a Bloodhound missile unit, 263 Sqn., was based at Watton, on the Griston side of the airfield.

After closure of the Station, administrative control was taken by RAF Honington. A few dedicated local townsfolk were determined that the sacrifices made by Watton's airmen in WW2 should not be forgotten and as a result a small museum was established, first in the old guardroom and later in the Officers' Mess. Featured are two memorials that stand outside the mess, one a Blenheim propellor salvaged from one of the aircraft lost in the fateful raid on Aalborg airfield in Denmark when eleven Blenheims of 82 Sqn. were shot down, virtually the whole squadron. Appropriately, this memorial was unveiled by Air Commodore Elworthy, a Commandant of The Queen's Flight, whose father MRAF Lord Elworthy, had served at Watton as CO of 82 Sqn. in those early days of the war.

OFFICIAL NAME - WATTON   LOCAL NAME - NEATON

COUNTY:	Norfolk	**AIRFIELD CODE:**	Wartime WN
LOCATION:	9.5 miles S.E. of Swaffham.	**OBSTACLES:**	Water Tower, Church
		LANDING:	11/29 6000ft. x 150ft.
LANDMARKS:	Griston church, S. of airfield.		concrete (from 1944)
		HOUSING:	Permanent
O/S-GRID REF:	TL999941 (centre of runway)	**HANGARS:**	4 type C; 2 type B1; 3 blister (airfield)
LAT:	53° 34' 10"N		3 type T2 grouped
LONG:	01° 52' 10"E		(3rd SAD site)
CONTROL TOWER:	1 - 'Fort' type 207/36	**OPENED :**	1939
	2 - Type 12779/41	**CLOSED:**	1988
	3 - modified by VCR type 5871c/55.	**CURRENT USE:**	DZ for para-dropping. (airfield)
HEIGHT ASL:	190ft		Prison (SAD site)
LIGHTING:	Mk.II		

UNITS PRESENT AT WATTON

UNIT	CODE	FROM	DATE IN	DATE OUT	TO	AIRCRAFT USED
21 Sqn.	UP	Eastchurch	2.3.39	24.6.40	Lossiemouth	Blenheim
34 Sqn.	LB	Upper Heyford	2.3.39	8.39	Singapore	Blenheim
82 Sqn.	UX	Cranfield	25.8.39	1.10.40	Bodney	Blenheim
18 Sqn.	GU/ WV	Crecy + Abbeville	20.5.40	26.5.40	Gatwick	Blenheim
105 Sqn.	GB	Honington	10.7.40	31.10.40	Swanton Morley	Blenheim
21 Sqn.	YH	Lossiemouth	29.10.40	27.5.41	Lossiemouth	Blenheim
90 Sqn.	WO	(re-formed)	7.5.41	15.5.41	West Raynham	Fortress
21 Sqn.	YH	Lossiemouth	14.6.41	17.7.41	Manston	Blenheim
21 Sqn.	YH	Manston	25.7.41	7.9.41	Lossiemouth	Blenheim
21 Sqn.	YH	Lossiemouth	21.9.41	26.12.41	Malta (Luqa)	Blenheim
1508 (BAT) Flt.		Horsham St. Faith	20.12.41	1.9.42	Horsham St. Faith	Blenheim
17(P)AFU		(formed)	29.1.42	6.11.42	Bodney	Master
17(P)AFU det.			6.11.42	5.43	Calveley	Master
406th BS	J6	Alconbury	2.44	3.44	Harrington	B-24
802nd RG		USA	22.4.44	9.8.44	to 25th BG (R)	B-17; B-24; Mosquito
25th BG (Recce)		(ex 802nd RG)	9.8.44	23.7.45	USA	B-17; B-24; B-26;
652nd BS	YN					P-38; Mosquito
653rd BS	WX					
654th BS	XN?					
Radio War. Est.	U3 4S, V7	Foulsham	27.9.45	1.9.46	(became CSE)	(various)
527 Sqn.	WN	Digby	8.11.45	15.4.46	(disbanded)	Spitfire; Oxford; Wellington; Dominie
Cent. Sigs. Est.	4S, V7	(ex RWE)	1.9.46	1.6.65	(disbanded)	(various)
751 Sqn.		(re-formed)	1.3.47	30.9.47	(disbanded)	Anson; Oxford; Seafire
192 Sqn.	DT	(re-formed)	15.7.51	21.8.58	(disbanded)	Lincoln; Washington; Canberra
199 Sqn.		(re-formed)	16.7.51	17.4.52	Hemswell	Lincoln; Mosquito
751 Sqn.		(re-formed)	3.12.51	31.1.57	Gibraltar	Mosquito; Sea Fury; Firefly; Anson; Avenger
116 Sqn.		(re-formed from Calibration N Sqn.)	1.8.52	21.8.58	(disbanded)	Lincoln; Anson; Varsity
527 Sqn.		(re-formed from Calibration R Sqn.)	1.8.52	21.8.58	(disbanded)	Lincoln; Canberra; Anson; Mosquito; Meteor; Varsity
815 Sqn.		HMS Illustrious	14.10.54	23.10.54	Ford	Avenger
751 Sqn.		Gibraltar	28.2.57	27.9.57	Culdrose	Avenger; Sea Venom
51 Sqn.		(re-formed)	21.8.58	31.3.63	Wyton	Canberra; Comet
115 Sqn.		(re-formed)	21.8.58	25.8.58	Tangmere	Valetta
245 Sqn.		(re-formed)	21.8.58	25.8.58	Tangmere	Canberra
263 Sqn.		(re-formed)	1.1.59	30.6.63	(disbanded)	Bloodhound missile
151 Sqn.		(re-formed from Development Sqn.)	1.1.62	25.5.63	(disbanded)	Hastings; Varsity; Canberra
97 Sqn.		(re-formed)	25.5.63	2.1.67	(disbanded)	Canberra; Varsity; Hastings
831 Sqn.		Culdrose	26.7.63	16.5.66	(disbanded)	Gannet; Sea Venom; Sea Vampire; Sea Prince
98 Sqn.		Tangmere	1.10.63	17.4.69	Cottesmore	Canberra
115 Sqn.		Tangmere	1.10.63	9.4.69	Cottesmore	Valetta; Argosy
360 Sqn.		(formed)	1.4.66	21.4.69	Cottesmore	Canberra
361 Sqn.		(formed)	2.1.67	14.7.67	(disbanded)	Canberra